I Am a Little Fashion Designer

Mayumi Oono

Let's design some clothes! Can you help me?

Thread rack

Back

Sewing machine

Serger

Workbench

Yardstick

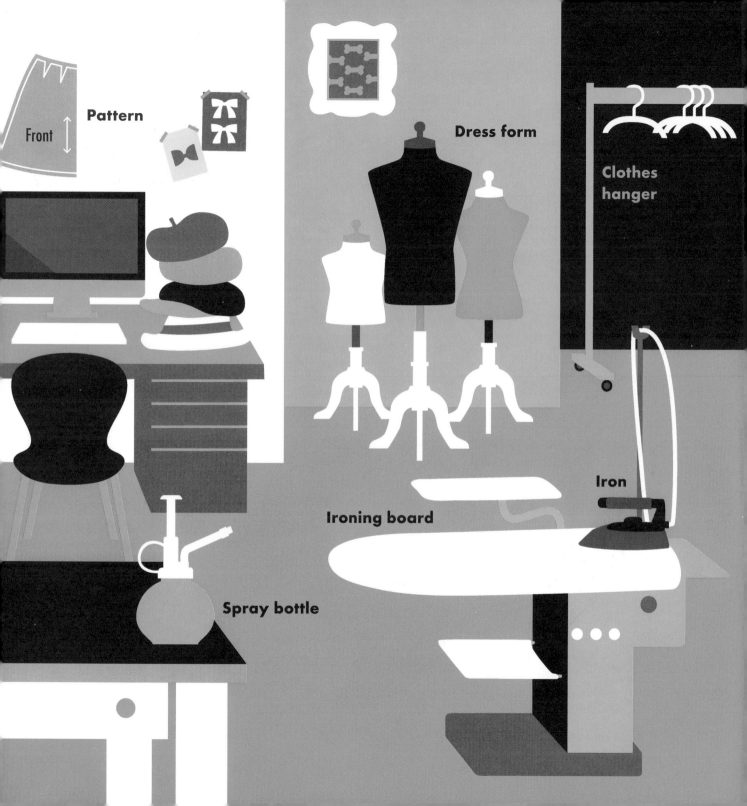

Pattern

Front

Dress form

Clothes hanger

Iron

Ironing board

Spray bottle

What design are we working on today?

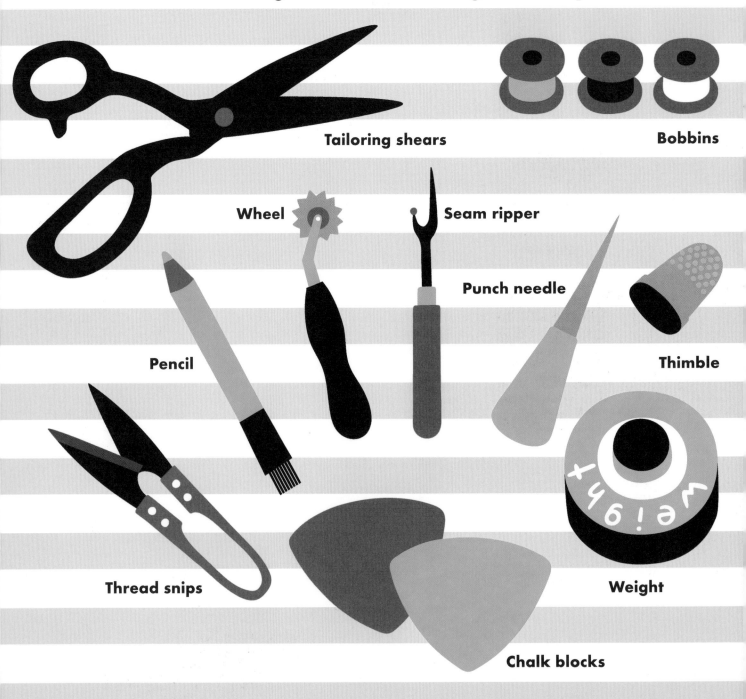

Tailoring shears

Bobbins

Wheel

Seam ripper

Punch needle

Pencil

Thimble

Thread snips

Weight

Chalk blocks

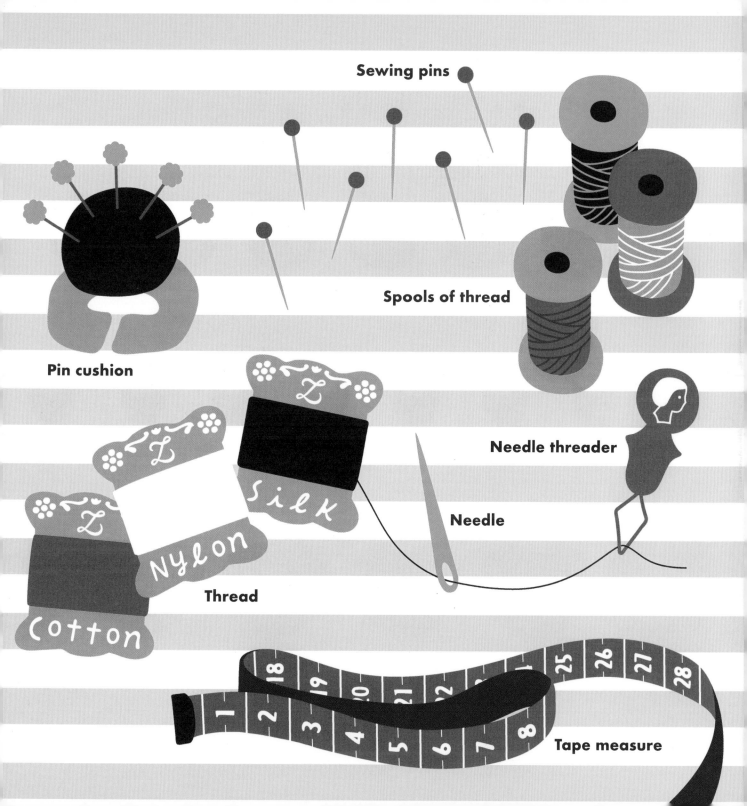

Sewing pins

Pin cushion

Spools of thread

Needle threader

Needle

Thread

Cotton

Nylon

Silk

Tape measure

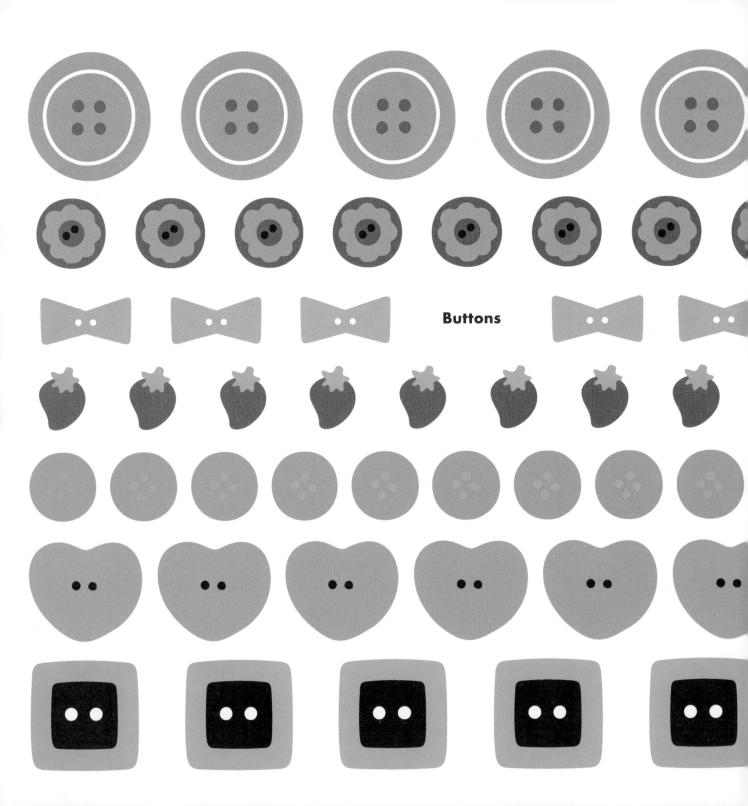

Buttons

Let's make a skirt!

1. Measure

2. Design

Skirt

weight

3. Make your pattern

Fabrics

Ribbons

Choosing materials—this is the fun part!

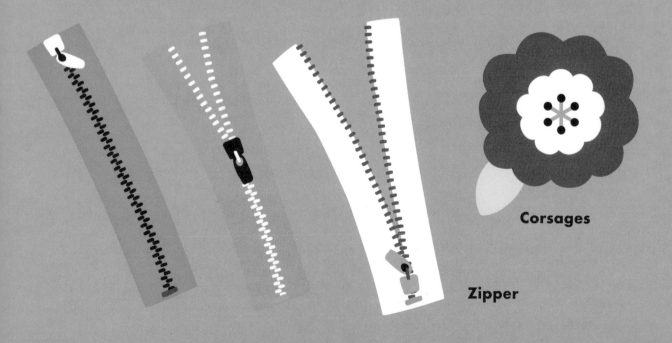

Corsages

Zipper

4. Cut

5. Sew

It's done!

The fashion show begins!

A floral pattern...

...a florist's apron!

A whipped-cream pattern...

...a pastry chef's uniform!

A pattern of musical notes...

...a musician's costume!

A pattern for puppies...

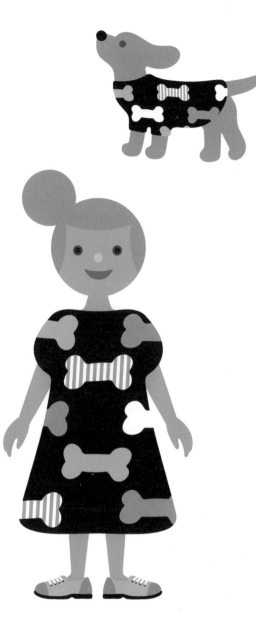

...a matching dress!

A hearts pattern...

...an artist's smock!

An ice-cream pattern...

...a dessert-lover's sweater!

Now, fashion doesn't end here.

Choose your clothes, put them on, and you're ready to go.

Mix and match, create your own outfits!

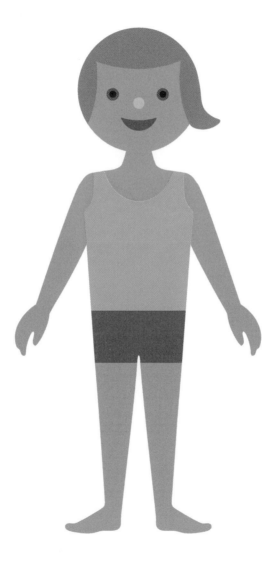

Special thanks to Keiko Hirai (Si-Si-Si comfort) and Ryuichi Sudo.—MO

Little Professionals: I Am a Little Fashion Designer first published
in the United States by Tra Publishing 2022.
Second Tra Publishing U.S. edition: March 2022.

Text, illustrations, and paper engineering © 2021 Mayumi Oono
Original edition © 2021 Zahorí Books, Barcelona (Spain)
Original title: *El meu petit taller de moda*

Printed and bound in China
ISBN: 978-1-7347618-5-6

Little Professionals: I Am a Little Fashion Designer is printed on Forest
Stewardship Council certified paper from well-managed forests.
Tra Publishing is committed to sustainability in its materials and practices.

Tra Publishing
245 NE 37th Street
Miami, FL 33137
trapublishing.com

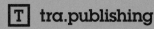

Now do it yourself!